GERMANY
WORLD ADVENTURES

BY EMMA CALWAY

KidHaven PUBLISHING

Published in 2018 by
KidHaven Publishing, an Imprint of Greenhaven Publishing, LLC
353 3rd Avenue
Suite 255
New York, NY 10010

Designer: Matt Rumbelow
Editor: Charlie Ogden

Cataloging-in-Publication Data

Names: Calway, Emma.
Title: Germany / Emma Calway.
Description: New York : KidHaven Publishing, 2018. | Series: World adventures | Includes glossary and index.
Identifiers: ISBN 9781534524101 (pbk.) | 9781534524088 (library bound) | ISBN 9781534525221 (6 pack) |
ISBN 9781534524095 (ebook)
Subjects: LCSH: Germany–Juvenile literature.
Classification: LCC DD17.C35 2018 | DDC 943–dc23

Printed in the United States of America

CPSIA compliance information: Batch #CW18KL: For further information contact Greenhaven Publishing LLC, New York, New York at 1-844-317-7404.

Please visit our website, www.greenhavenpublishing.com. For a free color catalog of all our
high-quality books, call toll free 1-844-317-7404 or fax 1-844-317-7405.

GERMANY

WORLD ADVENTURES

CONTENTS

Words in **red** can be found in the glossary on page 24.

WHERE IS GERMANY?

Germany is a large country in Europe. It has nine countries around it, including France, Austria, and Poland.

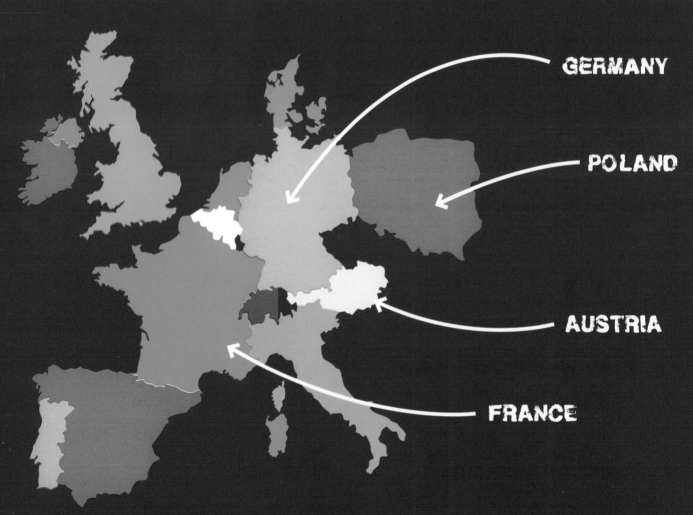

GERMANY

POLAND

AUSTRIA

FRANCE

Over 80 million people live in Germany. The capital city of Germany is Berlin.

WEATHER AND LANDSCAPE

In summer it gets very hot. The hottest months are usually June, July, and August. Germany often has cold winters with lots of snow.

Germany has many forests, rivers, and mountains. The longest river is called the Rhine. In winter, people go on holiday there.

People visit the mountains to go skiing.

THE RHINE

CLOTHING

Lederhosen are a type of **traditional** clothing worn by men in Germany. They come down to the knees and are worn with socks and shoes.

LEDERHOSEN

8

German women traditionally wore a long dress called a dirndl. Dirndls are worn with a white blouse and an apron.

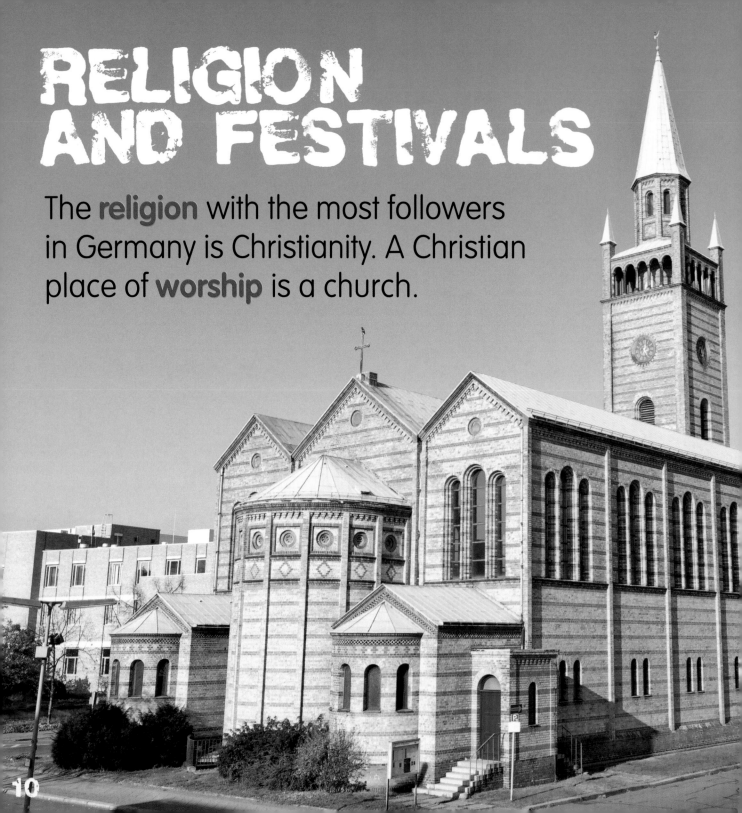

RELIGION AND FESTIVALS

The **religion** with the most followers in Germany is Christianity. A Christian place of **worship** is a church.

Oktoberfest is a **festival** that takes place in Germany every year. Men and women dress in lederhosen and dirndls and they often dance to music.

FOOD

Germans often eat meat as part of their main meal. Sauerbraten (sour roast) is one of the country's most popular dishes.

SAUERBRATEN

Germany is famous for its cakes.
After lunch, people sometimes
have a slice of cake and a coffee.

AT SCHOOL

Children in Germany go to school from six years old. Many schoolchildren get to school by walking or by taking the bus.

Children learn many subjects at school including German, math, science, and languages.
School often starts before 8 o'clock in the morning.

AT HOME

People in towns and cities in Germany usually live in tall apartment buildings. Around 3.5 million people live in Berlin.

In the villages there is more space. Many people live on farms and grow **crops**, such as wheat, barley, and corn.

WHEAT

CORN

BARLEY

17

FAMILIES

Families in Germany are very like families in the rest of Europe. Children usually live at home with their parents and **siblings**.

German families usually get together to celebrate special **occasions**, such as birthdays and holidays. They usually celebrate with cake and presents.

SPORTS

Tennis, motor racing, and soccer are all popular sports in Germany.

Many Germans go to sports clubs to play sports. Other popular sports include handball, basketball, and ice hockey.

The German soccer team has won four World Cups.

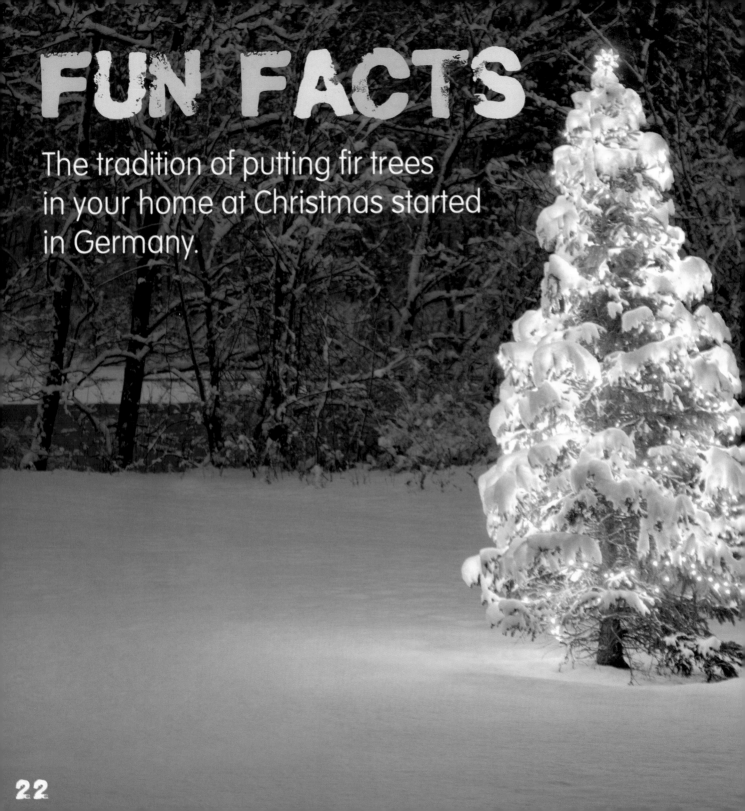

FUN FACTS

The tradition of putting fir trees in your home at Christmas started in Germany.

Germany's forests, the Black Forest and the Bavarian Forest, are home to wild boar, foxes, and deer.

DEER

WILD BOAR

GLOSSARY

crops
plants grown by farmers to make food for people

festival
a celebration of a special event or time of the year

occasions
special events

religion
the belief in and worship of a god or gods

siblings
brothers and sisters

traditional
ways of behaving that have been done for a long time

worship
a religious act, such as praying

INDEX